Hibernation

by Robin Nelson

first step nonfiction

Lerner Publications Company · Minneapolis

Snow covers the ground.

It is winter. Where are the animals?

Many animals are **hibernating**.

Hibernation is like a deep
sleep.

Hibernation is part of a **cycle**.

Animals hibernate to **survive** the winter.

They hibernate because it is
cold. They can't find food.

Snow hides plants and other food.

This bear sleeps in its **den**
in the winter.

In the spring, the bear will
wake up and come out.

Some snakes hibernate.

Most ground squirrels
hibernate.

Some bats hibernate.

Hedgehogs hibernate.

Many animals hibernate
every winter.

This cycle happens every year.

Learn More about Hibernation

Bears do not hibernate the same way as other animals do. Hibernating is different from sleeping. When animals hibernate, their heartbeat slows down. Their body cools. Hibernating animals are hard to wake up. But bears do not sleep as deeply as other hibernating animals. Their bodies do not cool down very much. They wake up often to eat. Then they go back to sleep.

Fun Facts

Some animals that hibernate sleep all winter long without waking up. Other animals that hibernate wake up during the winter to eat and then go back to sleep.

Animals that hibernate spend each fall eating and gathering food to last them through the long winter.

The only bird that hibernates is the common poorwill.

 Here are some other animals that hibernate—chipmunks, hamsters, skunks, bats, prairie dogs, frogs, lizards, snakes, turtles, and some insects like bees and ladybugs.

 Where do animals hibernate? Some animals hibernate underground in a burrow. Others find shelter in trees. Bears hibernate in a cave or den.

Glossary

 cycle – something that happens over and over again over time

 den – a safe, hidden place for a wild animal

 hibernating – sleeping or resting through the winter

 survive – stay alive

Index

The images in this book are used with the permission of: © Kristian Sekulic/Shutterstock Images, p. 2; © Pakhnyushchyy/Dreamstime.com, p. 3; © Joe McDonald/Visuals Unlimited/Getty Images, pp. 4, 22 (3rd from top); © George McCarthy/naturepl.com, p. 5; © Steve Hopkin/Taxi/Getty Images, pp. 6, 22 (1st from top); © age fotostock/SuperStock, pp. 7, 22 (4th from top); © Cameron Read/Taxi/Getty Images, p. 8; © Tom Murphy/SuperStock, p. 9; © Flirt/SuperStock, pp. 10, 22 (2nd from top); © Stephen J. Krasemann/Photographer's Choice/Getty Images, p. 11; © Tom McHugh/Photo Researchers, Inc., p. 12; © Charles P. George/Visuals Unlimited, Inc., p. 13; © Lynn M. Stone/naturepl.com, p. 14; © Mike Birkhead/Photolibrary/Getty Images, p. 15; © Bob Elsdale/The Image Bank/Getty Images, p. 16; © Eric Baccega/naturepl.com, p. 17; © Igor Shpilenok/naturepl.com, p. 18.

Cover: © Charles P. George/Visuals Unlimited, Inc.

Lerner Publications Company
A division of Lerner Publishing Group, Inc.
241 First Avenue North
Minneapolis, MN 55401 U.S.A.

Website address: www.lernerbooks.com

Library of Congress Cataloging-in-Publication Data

Nelson, Robin, 1971–
        Hibernation / by Robin Nelson.
            p.   cm. — (First step nonfiction. Discovering nature's cycles)
        Includes index.
        ISBN 978–0–7613–4579–4 (lib. bdg. : alk. paper)
            1. Hibernation—Juvenile literature. I. Title.
    QL755.N45 2011
    591.56'5—dc22   2009020609

Manufactured in the United States of America
1 – DP – 7/15/10